peace at home

Simple Solutions for Serene Rooms

Juliet Pegrum

CHRONICLE BOOKS

SAN FRANCISCO

First published in the United States in 2003 by

Chronicle Books LLC.

Copyright © 2003 Duncan Baird Publishers. Text copyright © 2003 by Juliet Pegrum. For copyright of photographs see page 176, which is to be regarded as an extension of this copyright. All rights reserved. No part of this book may be reproduced in any form without written permission from the publisher.

Conceived, created, and designed

by Duncan Baird Publishers Ltd.

Sixth Floor, Castle House

75-76 Wells Street

London W1T 3QH

Library of Congress Cataloging-in-Publication Data available.

ISBN: 0-8118-3992-3

Manufactured in Thailand

Cover design by Eun Young Lee

Distributed in Canada by Raincoast Books

9050 Shaughnessy Street

Vancouver, British Columbia V6P 6E5

10 9 8 7 6 5 4 3 2 1

Chronicle Books LLC

85 Second Street

San Francisco, California 94105

www.chroniclebooks.com

"To my mother for all her kindness and for

providing my first experience of home."

contents

introduction

When we say we feel "at home," we are referring not simply to our physical location, but also to a state of being—to a sense of peacefulness in which we are free from troubling thoughts and emotions, where we are present in the moment and at one with ourselves. Of course, our state of being is influenced by our surroundings. In many modern environments we are constantly subjected to a barrage of sensory stimuli. As a result our minds grow stressed and anxious, our emotions volatile, and it becomes increasingly difficult to find the still point within ourselves. Attempting to cope with the overload, our senses contract, leading to experiences of isolation and separation from others and our surroundings. To assure well-being and happiness in modern life, it is imperative to create homes that are in tune with our senses, needs, and desires; that offer respite from the chaos and confusion of the outside world.

I conduct my work as an interior designer with the aim of creating such harmony in the homes of my clients. However, it is only in recent years that this aim has been consciously articulated. When I began my career, fresh out of graduate school, I was preoccupied with esthetics on the one hand, and on the other with a more general concern about the destruction of the environment by mass industry. In the years that followed, I pursued these interests through research into indigenous craft traditions and natural dyes. This in turn led to collaboration with a design company in India that works to conserve and promote the local craft traditions of the northern state of Rajasthan.

It was during one of my many visits to India that I came across Vastu—the ancient Indian art of architecture and design. It was this discovery that crystallized my concerns for the environment into an understanding of the symbiotic relationship that exists between our surroundings and our state of being: we affect the environment, and it, in turn, affects us. Therefore to create harmony in our surroundings is to promote health and well-being in our lives.

In writing this book it is my hope that I can help you to create homes that are not simply beautiful, but also in harmony with yourself. Drawing on the theories of Eastern philosophy, I offer some simple principles for designing interiors to soothe and nurture the spirit, fostering calm and inner peacefulness. The home is but a microcosm of the world: by bringing balance to our homes we take the first steps toward creating harmony in the world at large.

"In order for a person to
reach the highest state
of being, he or she must
first create a perfect world
in which to reach this
highest state."

Choney Lama

PRINCIPLES FOR A
PEACEFUL HOME

the art of peaceful living

A state of peacefulness is a feeling of being at home, of being at one with ourselves and the world. The current Western preoccupation with finding peacefulness stems from a pervasive sense of dissatisfaction and conflict, a feeling of disconnection and alienation from others and our surroundings. This separation between self and world is manifested in our tendency to see the home as an object entirely separate from the self, an attitude that fails to recognize the impact of our surroundings at all levels of consciousness: physical, mental, emotional, and spiritual. In interior design this attitude has led to the creation of living spaces that are esthetically pleasing but that ultimately fail to meet our deepest needs and desires.

Eastern traditions have long recognized the relationship of mutuality that exists between ourselves and our surroundings, for they believe self, home, and world to be inextricably connected, seeing them alike as manifestations of the fundamental unity of the universe. Working on this basis Eastern principles of interior design aim to promote balance and harmony between inner and outer worlds so that the home becomes an extension of the body, a vehicle for the spirit. It is believed that when this is achieved we take the first steps toward inner peace as we discover a sense of wholeness and a feeling of connection with the world around us.

Harmonious living environments are those that fulfill our needs and desires. This chapter looks at seven key principles of interior design that help us to create such living spaces. Our most basic need is for space—space in which to live, to breathe, and to grow. Consequently the first of these principles is concerned with the balance between space and form within the home, for this determines the way that we move through and interact with our living environment. The next three principles concern the use of materials, color, and light, and are based on a recognition that we relate to our environment primarily through our five senses—the doorways of perception. If this relationship is to be harmonious, our interiors must be pleasing to the senses —not simply comfortable, but stimulating or soothing, with rich textures, melodious sounds, and color and lighting schemes that are appropriate to the atmosphere of the room. Underlying these concrete principles are abstract principles of balance, simplicity, and unity. These help us to coordinate our use of space, materials, color, and light to create interiors that are in tune with both ourselves and the world we live in.

space and form

Our most basic need is for space. When we clutter up our homes with an excess of possessions and overly elaborate decoration, we create interiors that, far from being peaceful, inhibit free movement and distract the mind. To transform our homes into more calming environments, the first step is to strike a balance between clear space and objects or decoration. The ancient philosophies of China and Japan conceive of this balance in terms of the heaven principle (represented by an empty room) and the earth principle (represented by the physical objects that occupy a room). Humans exist in relation to the principles of heaven and earth: where there is balance between the two in our immediate environment (a balance between space and form), we live in a state of harmony—able to move, breathe, and think with freedom, ease, and contentment.

The first step toward attaining this balance is to strip away all that is unnecessary in terms of decoration and material possessions. This is an act that focuses our minds on the space itself rather than on the structural elements of the room, such as walls, floors, doors, and windows. The result is a three-dimensional blank canvas in which we can bring together the separate elements

of color, texture, light, and form to create a unified and harmonious whole.

In modern urban environments where space is an expensive luxury, finding a balance between space and form can be a problem—many people are forced to live in small houses and apartments, whose rooms are often dark, cramped, and claustrophobic. To create the illusion of space in such homes, it is important to maximize the flow of natural light. Where extensive structural changes are possible, this can be achieved by knocking rooms together to produce one large room, inserting openings in the connecting walls of two rooms, enlarging windows, or, in loft rooms, installing skylights.

Simpler approaches include painting walls and ceilings in pale, light-reflective colors and introducing additional overhead lighting and free-standing lamps.

The size of a room closely affects the choice and placement of furniture, ornaments, and decorative elements. In addition to choosing furniture that is proportionate in size to the space, you can foster a greater sense of openness by keeping the center of your interiors free from obstruction. This is an important principle of Eastern design, founded on the belief that the center of a room equates to the heart and should therefore be kept open to allow the free flow of energy through the space.

materials

The nature of the materials used in a home influence our sensory experience in terms of touch, sight, and sound and therefore play a crucial role in the creation of a peaceful interior. Of all the senses touch is our primary mode of perception—we develop a sense of touch as unborn babies, well before our ears register sound or our eyes begin to focus on external forms and colors. One aspect of touch is sensitivity to temperature. If our interiors are to feel comfortable, we must maintain them at a constant ambient temperature. The materials we use to decorate them can help us to achieve this aim. In cold climates use heavy fabrics, such as linen, heavy cottons, and raw silk for soft furnishings; and thick carpets or matting on the floors, to provide insulation. To reduce the temperature in hot climates, choose materials that conduct heat, such as stone, ceramics, glass, and steel, for flooring, walls, and other surfaces; and use thin, light fabrics, such as muslin, fine cottons, silk, and taffeta, for drapes and upholstery.

When selecting materials for an interior, it is also important to consider the function of the room. In spaces geared toward relaxation, soothing textures are most appropriate. For

example, in a bedroom you could induce an atmosphere of warmth and comfort with cushions and throws made from soft, luxurious fabrics, such as velvet, lambswool, and mohair; elegant wooden furniture with a smooth, silky grain; and thick carpets or fluffy rugs underfoot. Conversely, in rooms where there is a constant flurry of activity, a more stimulating combination of different textures is appropriate. For example, in the kitchen shown on the previous page, the roughness of the wooden table, the carved bowls, and the fireplace mantel contrast sharply with the smooth, white, streamlined chairs, the refined, white china bowls, and the cool, smooth stone of the floor. Such textural contrasts also appeal to our sense of sight, bringing life and energy into the interior by banishing the visual monotony of uniform surfaces.

As well as influencing our senses of touch and sight, the types of materials used in an interior influence our auditory environment. Thick carpets and opulent drapes, upholstered furniture, and an abundance of cushions and throws absorb sound, creating a subdued environment appropriate to relaxation in a bedroom. Hard surfaces, such as tiled, stone, or wooden floors, and slatted blinds bounce sound around a living space, making for a noisier environment that is better suited to activity-oriented rooms, such as kitchens and dining rooms.

In visual terms natural rather than manmade materials tend to be the most beautiful, varied, and interesting. This is because, unlike the uniformity of synthetic materials, every slab of stone, strip of wood, or sheet of metal is unique, bearing individual patterns of color, grain, and patina. Furthermore, natural materials age gracefully, becoming more interesting as time passes: angular stone steps develop intriguing curves where they have been worn smooth by footsteps; the rugged grain of wood acquires a polished luster; reddish copper takes on a green, weather-beaten tinge; and the colors of naturally dyed fabrics soften when exposed to sunlight.

Beyond their esthetic appeal it is their inherent connection with nature that makes natural materials essential features of peaceful interiors. Eastern traditions, such as Japanese Shintoism, believe that all the elements of the natural world, from the tallest tree to the smallest grain of sand, possess a life or vibration of their own. The vibrations of these natural elements are believed to harmonize with our own energies, promoting balance and peace within the home. Manmade substances tend to lack these qualities and in some cases even have a toxic effect on our environment. Formica and other molded plastics are examples of such substances because they contain harmful chemicals, such as benzene and formaldehyde, that degrade the air quality.

color

Color has a profound impact on our visual experience of an interior and is therefore a vitally important design tool that we can manipulate to create a soothing or stimulating atmosphere in any room of the home. In scientific terms each color is a dimension of white light, which is made up of energy waves of varying lengths that together form a visible spectrum or rainbow. Each color corresponds to a particular wavelength: red, at the warmer end of the spectrum, has the longest wavelength; violet, at the cooler end of the spectrum, has the shortest. When particular wavelengths of light fall on the retina (the light-sensitive region at the back of the eye), a message is transmitted to the brain, which interprets the waves as a particular color.

Every color, or wave of light energy, has a direct physiological and psychological impact on the state of our minds and bodies. Cooler colors are more calming; warmer colors more stimulating. For example, red—the hottest color—has been scientifically proven to increase heart rate. When choosing a color scheme for an interior, it is therefore important to consider the effects that particular colors have. Red is associated with fire and stimulates passion and desire;

orange is linked with spiritual endeavor and promotes transcendence; yellow represents sunlight and encourages optimism; green connects us to nature and promotes harmony; blue is associated with the sky, suggesting openness; indigo recalls the ocean depths and adds mystery; violet symbolizes the "inner eye", the center for spiritual vision—and is believed to encourage introspection.

In India not only the color itself but also the tone and the intensity of the color—whether it is bright, dark, or light—are thought to have physiological repercussions. Splashes of hot, bright color excite the senses, sparking restlessness and activity. Dark tints, such as

brown, indigo, and maroon, carry a heaviness that gives rootedness and depth but causes lethargy in excess. Pale colors are the most calming, as they have a high proportion of white and therefore a balance of all the colors.

Deciding on a specific mood suited to the function of the space is the first step when determining the color palette for an interior. For example, if you wanted to create a sense of expansion in a bedroom, you might use shades of blue set against a calming white background (above). In a living room you might develop a color scheme combining cheerful yellow to encourage social interaction, with earthier colors, such as chocolate brown and soft purple, to give a grounding effect (opposite).

When combining a number of disparate colors in this way, it is important to match colors of similar tones; schemes containing many different colors in a variety of tones are

visually disturbing. To create a balanced, harmonious effect, use either a range of colors in matching tones or a restricted number of colors in different tones and shades. A safe option is to choose monochromes, such as shades of cream, off white, buff, or gray, for your base colors. Such neutral hues do not clash and therefore provide a good backdrop for splashes of livelier color.

A great illusionist, color alters the visual dimensions of a living space. Therefore your approach should be geared to the particular shape and size of your interior. For example, if you are decorating a small room, a pale color scheme will make it seem larger. In a large, airy space, painting the walls in warmer tones will help to create a cozier effect. If a ceiling is disproportionately high when compared with the size of the room, painting the ceiling in a dark shade will make it seem lower.

light and dark

In addition to color, the balance and interplay of light and dark are instrumental in shaping our visual experience of our environment. To promote harmony and well-being within our homes, it is essential to create a balance of light and shade in each interior that is appropriate to the room's function at different times of the day.

Light has an energizing effect on the body, promoting activity and mental alertness; an abundance of light is therefore desirable in rooms that are used for active daytime pursuits. Natural light comprises the full spectrum of colors and is the most energizing form of light—lack of exposure results in vitamin D deficiencies and can induce depression, fatigue, irritability, and hormonal imbalances. It is therefore better to live in living spaces that have too much light than too little. If your home is relatively dark, you can increase the amount of natural light with reflective surfaces, such as mirrors, to bounce the light around each room.

In rooms that host the relaxed activities of evening and night-time, it is often fitting to create more shaded environments that will subdue the conscious mind in readiness for sleep.

This can be achieved by window treatments that control the amount of natural light entering a space. Thick drapes and shutters enable you to shut out natural light completely, providing a cocoon of darkness that is ideal for the bedroom. Blinds, voiles, and translucent shades (opposite) limit the amount of light entering a room without blocking it out entirely; these are better suited to rooms, such as the living room and dining room, where they foster an atmosphere of seclusion and intimacy perfect for gatherings of family and friends.

Artificial lighting schemes offer us much greater control over the balance of light and shade in interiors, and can be used to enhance or compensate for the incipient effects of natural light. To create a vibrant daytime environment, particularly in rooms that are lacking in natural light, install full-spectrum overhead lighting—small, discreet spotlights are ideal because they give a diffused effect, akin to natural daylight. In rooms where a more restful atmosphere is desired, devise a lighting scheme based on a combination of low-wattage lamps and uplighters to produce soothing patterns of light and shade. Experiment with incandescent lightbulbs. These emit light predominating in red and yellow wavelengths, delivering a soft, rosy glow. For a more temporary arrangement, switch off the main lights and light some candles: with their gently

flickering radiance, these produce a particularly relaxing and romantic effect.

The key to a good lighting scheme is a level of flexibility that allows you to accommodate a broad spectrum of human activities, from the more relaxed to the very active. This is particularly important in multifunctional interiors, such as open-plan living spaces, where a single living space hosts a range of different activities. To achieve such flexibility use a combination of different light fittings, with dimmable wall-lights or overhead spotlights teamed with a selection of portable lamps positioned strategically to draw attention to areas of activity and interaction.

balance

A sense of balance is fundamental to a peaceful interior. It is a principle that applies generally to the use of materials, colors, light, and shade, and has particular relevance to the placement of furniture. Symmetry is a type of strict visual balance established when two or more identical objects are placed on either side of a dividing line (real or imaginary) to form mirror-images (opposite). Symmetry is present in many natural forms and reflects the inherent harmony of nature. By applying symmetry to the layout or decoration of a room, we produce a general feeling of balance and rest.

Asymmetry brings balance without the need for mirror-imaging. An example would be the placement of two differently shaped objects at opposite ends of a mantelpiece. Alternatively, two objects of different sizes can be balanced around a central axis according to their position, with larger objects closer to the axis and smaller ones farther away. For example, if you had two paintings of different sizes, you would bring them into balance by hanging the larger of the two toward the central axis of your wall, and the smaller painting farther out. Asymmetry is often used in Eastern interiors and has a more dynamic effect than formal symmetry.

simplicity

One of the key principles governing the design of Eastern interiors is simplicity—a conscious stripping away of all that is inessential. This asceticism stems from a desire to bring the mind into an enlightened state of clarity, to a focused awareness, where it is no longer distracted by the illusory multiplicity of the world, and can instead move toward an apprehension of the underlying unified reality of the cosmos.

The principle of simplicity can be applied to any interior to create an atmosphere of peace in which the mind and body can rest, undisturbed by the constant barrage of stimuli that flood the senses in the outside world. In practice this involves the avoidance of overly elaborate decoration and the removal of any unnecessary possessions so that only objects and furnishings of true function, beauty, or personal value remain. In the context of a simple interior, the unique qualities of individual items are appreciated much more keenly. For example, a dark painting and twisted willow branches arranged in a pot seem more striking and beautiful when set against the simplicity of bare white walls and a pale wooden floor (opposite).

unity

Eastern philosophies hold that a fundamental unity exists within all of creation—a unity based not on a static sameness, but on the constantly changing, dynamic interplay between polar opposites. This philosophy is conveyed by the ancient Chinese black and white *yin/yang* symbol, an image whose rotational symmetry suggests continuous cyclic movement. This oneness manifests itself as a balance between complementary opposites, for it is only through the interplay of difference that distinctions can be made: there can be no day without night, no summer without winter, no life without death, no light without dark.

A sense of dynamic unity is an essential feature of a peaceful interior, for it brings the space into harmony with not only ourselves, but also the cosmos as a whole. In design terms this principle involves maintaining a balance between contrasting opposites: for example, between the opposing colors of black and white, and the contrasting patterns of striped fabric and a mottled floor (opposite left); between the varied textures of smooth cotton cushions and rough wicker baskets, and different materials, such as warm wood and cold stone (opposite right).

A unified design can also develop from an overriding vision that reflects the self—perhaps an equestrian theme to express an interest in horseriding, a bold color scheme to mirror a playful personality. Above all, your home should be at one with your interior world—your personality, desires, needs, and interests. When this occurs the distinctions between inner and outer merge, resulting in a profound sense of connection with the world.

"Life nourishes

Environment shapes

Influences complete."

Lao Zi

LIVING ROOMS

social spaces

The living room is the nucleus or spiritual heart of the home. It is a space of diverse activities—the perfect setting for social gatherings and a haven of relaxation at the end of a busy day. The largest and airiest of your living spaces is the obvious location for such activities. If your living room is relatively small, consider knocking through into an adjacent room, such as the dining room or entrance hall. This will extend the living room into the rest of the home, creating a more relaxed and expansive effect. Living rooms are used predominantly in the evenings, so the ideal location is in the west of the home—the aspect that receives the warm rays of the setting sun.

In terms of layout leave the center of the room open and generous to embrace visitors into the space as they enter. Try to keep unnecessary furniture and clutter to a minimum to allow freedom of movement throughout the room. Retain only items that serve a vital function, and ornaments and artifacts that bring you real pleasure—others are merely a distraction.

Sofas and chairs are typically the largest and most important pieces of furniture in the living room. They should be comfortable with soft, rounded forms that encourage rest and repose. Orient them around the warm hearth of a fireplace (if you have one), or arrange them in a group to encourage lively social interaction. The ideal distance between chairs is anywhere between four and ten feet (one to three meters). Distances greater than ten feet leave guests feeling distant and disconnected from each other; those less than four feet risk compromising personal space.

Introduce a flexible lighting scheme that accommodates the assorted activities of the room. Dimmable overhead spotlights enable you to have bright lighting for large parties, and low lighting for more intimate gatherings. A variety of uplighters or lamps positioned strategically throughout the room will make soft pools of light amid shadows—perfect for romantic trysts or solitary activities such as reading.

comfort

A comfortable living room is one that soothes body, mind, and spirit, fostering a perfect state of balance on all levels of existence. To generate a sense of comfort in your living room, create a perfect balance between open spaces (which permit free movement), and clusters of furniture (such as easy chairs, sofas, and floor cushions on which you and your guests can relax). Choose your sofa with particular care. This is likely to be the main piece of furniture in the living room and will provide a place to rest after the rigors of the day. A truly comfortable sofa is one that is soft yet supportive, molding to the human form like a glove so that the body feels weightless and

free from pressure. In terms of size your sofa should be long enough to allow you to stretch out fully, but not so large that it dominates the room. Sofas that are relatively deep with high arms (left) are suitable if you prefer to curl up when sitting. Adorn furniture with the soft volumes of scatter cushions and cozy, textured throws made of lambswool, alpaca, or mohair.

Introduce curved shapes into your interior to soothe the eye and soften any hard geometric architectural lines—perhaps a classic rocking chair in the corner, a circular table by a chair, or a simple rounded vase on the sideboard. Such shapes create a warm, sensuous, and inviting living environment. They appeal to our tactile, comfort-loving natures beckoning us to nestle in the arms of an easy chair, to recline along the length of a chaise longue.

organic forms

Most of us spend almost ninety per cent of our lives indoors (whether at work or at home). As a result, those of us living in urban landscapes are almost entirely cut off from nature—our source of spiritual nourishment and support—and it is not surprising that many suffer from feelings of depression and isolation. To correct this imbalance we need to reconnect with nature through our interiors. We can begin by softening the clean, straight lines of human-made structures with the gentle, soothing curves that are intrinsic to organic forms. Echo the rounded form of a leaf with a gently curving chair (opposite); take inspiration from the fluid patterns of waves by draping fabrics loosely over surfaces; invoke glistening pools of water with oval mirrors and round glass bowls.

"Things grow and grow. But each goes back to its root. Going back to the root is stillness. This means returning to what is. Returning to what is means going back to the ordinary."

Lao Zi

Incorporating natural materials into your furnishings is another way to bring organic forms into your home. Try wooden floorboards, cool marble or rough seagrass matting underfoot. Leave brick walls and wooden beams exposed to draw attention to the natural fabric of the building. Alternatively, adorn your living room with relics of the outdoors—roughly hewn logs stored in a tin bucket (previous page), smooth pebbles displayed in simple bowls (following page), delicate feathers arranged on a tray (below).

The Japanese believe that images of organic forms are soothing to the spirit. Follow their example by filling your living room with objects that recall the bounty of nature—an elegant arrangement of paper flowers, a silk screen decorated with pictures of trees and birds.

Plants or beautiful flower arrangements bring the sights and scents of the natural world directly into the home. If your living room is bright with lively colors, choose flowers that blend in with the color scheme. In a minimalist interior inject a splash of color with some vividly colored blooms. Alternatively, you could opt for muted arrangements of brushwood or grasses (opposite) that are in keeping with the simplicity of the decor.

The impulse to adorn our living spaces began with the birth of human civilization, when we first developed the ability to think and communicate using images and symbols. Since the first cave paintings produced by our prehistoric ancestors, humans have sought to express themselves and their relation to the world through their immediate surroundings. To do so effectively is to bring the home into harmony with the self so that it becomes an extension of the body and a haven for the spirit.

The ornaments with which we decorate our homes provide a delightful means of expressing our individuality, for they are versatile and portable—allowing us to alter the look of rooms according to our current moods and tastes. The addition of a bold painting (opposite), an arrangement of natural forms (right), or striking abstract wall sculptures (following page) transforms plain interiors by providing focal points for the eye.

Alternatively, particularly beautiful or inspiring artifacts—perhaps a tribal mask brought back from

ornamentation

"Things are objects where there is a subject or mind;

and the mind is a subject where there are objects."

Sosan Zenji

Africa or a silk screen from China—can supply a unifying theme for an interior as a whole, around which all the other elements of the room are coordinated.

Display objects that have meaning or value to you, such as a boat sculpture (above) if you enjoy sailing. Avoid harsh shapes, discordant colors, or images or objects depicting violent scenes, for these will disturb the harmony of your interior. When selecting your ornaments you should also consider how well they work together. It is possible to mix pieces of varying styles and from different periods, provided there is a common element that links them—perhaps specific colors and shapes, or contrasts between opposites, such as rough and smooth, light and dark. Choose objects that harmonize with the room. Small framed pictures work better in more intimate spaces—they can become lost in larger rooms, which suit big pieces or groups of smaller works.

raw elements

In Vedic philosophy it is believed that all physical matter is composed of five raw elements: Ether, Air, Water, Fire, and Earth. By bringing representatives of these elements into the living room, we help to balance them within our bodies, achieving inner and outer harmony.

An abundance of space is sufficient to promote the Ether element, while the textured surfaces of natural materials (above right) encourage Air, and a bowl of water or a fountain stimulates Water. As the living room forms the spiritual, if not literal, heart of the home, it is particularly important to encourage Fire, which is equated with spirit or energy. The flicker of firelight emanating from an open fireplace is the most obvious way to stimulate Fire, although lighting candles has a similar effect. If you have a fireplace, try burning some pine needles or aromatic herbs. These will give out a delicious earthy scent that also brings Earth into the interior.

"In the boundless space of suchness

In the play of the great light

All the miracles of sight, sound

   and mind."

Chogyam Trungpa

visual expansion

Living rooms with large windows and doors extend the gaze beyond the interior space, allowing the mind to wander and become spacious. A beautiful view of nature imbues an interior with serenity and peace, whether it overlooks rolling hills or a small urban garden. Open seascapes (right below), landscapes, even lawns, are especially calming because their horizontal lines communicate a sense of expansion and repose that is relaxing to the mind. Pathways that meander into the distance kindle an atmosphere of mystery and wonder that releases the imagination.

Within your interior arrange the seating to embrace the best vistas. To create a feeling of openness in small apartments without gardens, punctuate interior walls with windows or keyholes that look through into other areas of the home. Alternatively, conjure the illusion of space by decorating walls with landscape paintings or trompe l'oeil murals.

"Food is the principal
factor that materially
contributes to the
strength, complexion
and vitality of human
beings."

Gopi Warrier
and Deepika Gunawant

KITCHENS AND DINING ROOMS

nourishing spaces

The kitchen and dining room together represent the warm hearth of the home, the source of nourishment and vitality where food is prepared and consumed. They are communal spaces in which family and friends gather to participate in the act of eating, and as such they are associated with both physical and emotional comfort.

With its bustle of cooking and washing, the kitchen is one of the most active of living spaces. Reflect this in a design scheme that stimulates the senses, perhaps with bold, exciting colors, strong textural contrasts, and the fragrant aromas of herbs and fresh flowers. To promote stress-free cooking your kitchen should be well-designed in functional terms, with plenty of storage space together with ample room for maneuvering between the cooker, sink, and refrigerator units.

Ideally the kitchen should have plenty of access for sunlight, as this helps to dry up any condensation that forms during cooking. In addition to overhead lighting, install strip- or spotlights beneath wall-mounted cupboards to shed light on shaded worksurfaces. An extractor fan is also helpful for removing stale smells and steam from the kitchen.

Dedicated to the consumption of food, dining rooms should possess an atmosphere of relaxed conviviality that enhances our digestion and our enjoyment of the meal so that we gain maximum physical and emotional benefit from the experience. Walls painted in calming colors induce relaxation, while splashes of brighter colors in flower arrangements and tableware stimulate the appetite. If your dining area is located within your kitchen, try to create some separation between the area where you prepare the food and the area where you eat it—perhaps with a breakfast counter or screen, or a lighting scheme that allows you to dim the lights in one area and raise the lights in the other—so that the stimulating energies of the kitchen are kept apart from the relaxed energies of the dining room.

function and form

Kitchens that are both attractive and functional provide the
most relaxing cooking environments. In a well-designed
kitchen there should be plenty of storage space, with items,
such as the cooker, sink, and refrigerator, positioned within
easy reach of each other. Arranging them in an L- or U-
shaped layout is ideal, although in practice your layout will
depend on the size and shape of the space available. Typically
units are placed against walls, but in large kitchens a free-
standing worktop makes better use of space.

Your choice of work-surface has a big impact on the look
of your kitchen as well as on your enjoyment of the room as a
functional space. For a warm, rustic effect try seasoned wood

surfaces. If ease of cleaning is a priority, opt for a versatile laminate; although often disparaged as a cheaper option, when teamed with matching cupboards laminates can produce a look that is both sleek and sophisticated (below left).

Try to avoid the monotony of plain rows of cupboards by alternating open and closed units. In the closed units hide unattractive items, such as packets of food, and in the open or glass-fronted cupboards display elegant stacks of china, colorful spices, or matching vessels filled with dry foods. Make space for a shelf on which to store cookery books (opposite), and hang metal implements, pots, and pans on a rack next to the window where they will refract light around the kitchen (below right).

"When the opposites
arise, the Buddha
mind is lost."

Zen saying

Juxtaposing contrasting textures and colors will bring life and warmth to your kitchen—a softness and sensuousness that is sometimes missing from very functional kitchens. In stainless-steel kitchens temper the cold sheen of metal surfaces with displays of warmer-toned metal objects, such as brass bowls and copper pans. Alternatively, display simple ceramic bowls filled with brightly colored fruits, such as oranges and lemons (opposite). If you have tiled, glass, or polished granite work-surfaces, partner these with wooden cupboards and some roughly hewn earthenware pots to bring warmth to the interior. If there are exposed beams or brick walls in your kitchen, create an interplay of matte and shiny textures by replacing the door with a metal screen, or erecting some glass shelves (left)

vision and contrast

sensual stimulation

Transforming each mealtime into a feast for the eyes as well as the tastebuds enhances appreciation and enjoyment of the food. According to Vedic philosophy, by activating your sense of sight you encourage the Fire element, which stimulates appetite and promotes good digestion.

Present food on colorful dishes that either match or contrast with the colors of the ingredients: vibrant red and yellow peppers on deep blue plates; frosted pink ice cream in pretty white bowls. You could also take inspiration from the colors of your food when selecting napkins, tablecloths, and tablemats: citrus colors work well with bright salads; earthier tones complement the warmth of root vegetables. Place candles or a striking display of flowers or fruits in the center of the table—perhaps a row of small matching glass vases filled with violets, or a shallow ceramic bowl heaped with ripe oranges. If you have a sideboard, open cupboard or dresser in the dining room, use its surfaces to display beautiful crockery, glassware, or flowers.

conviviality

Eating in the company of family and friends in an atmosphere of relaxed conviviality is a delightful way to unwind at the end of a busy day. All you need is a light, open area that can accommodate a large table and a matching set of comfortable chairs. Walls painted in neutral shades offer the greatest flexibility, allowing you to vary the colors of place settings and table decorations to suit the nature of the meal. Cream, beige, and biscuit can produce warm, intimate atmospheres; cool shades of white, pale green, and gray are calming and create a sense of openness and expansion.

To bring humor and fun to social gatherings, introduce bold geometric shapes and splashes of bright color into the dining room with a set of modern triangular chairs combined with cubed

vases containing exuberant arrangements of tulips (page 74). For greater visual impact use the brilliant colors of flowers to inject a single dash of color into a monochrome interior (opposite).

To encourage profundity at an intimate evening meal, introduce subtle hints of deep mauve, purple, and blue into flower arrangements and tableware (left). If you desire light, witty conversation, opt for flashes of yellows and oranges. Display your flowers with careful consideration for the overall effect: simple arrangements of single stems, such as alliums (previous page) or arum lilies in tall vases (opposite), add a touch of modern sophistication to any dining room; a spray of lavender in a large glass vase gives a more casual impression.

The dining table is crucial to the overall look and feel of a dining area: antique oak exudes the rustic charm of a farmhouse table; pale, untreated ash conveys a simple austerity; translucent glass a cool sophistication. According to Vedic philosophy, not only the substance but also the shape of the table affects the ambiance of the room: square or rectangular tables represent the Earth element and thus have a grounding effect, whereas circular or oval tables symbolize the Water element, stimulating lively interaction.

"In this world of dreams,

dozing off once more;

still speaking

and dreaming of dreams.

Just let it be."

Ryokan

BEDROOMS

quiet spaces

A third of our lives is spent asleep. If we are to function effectively during the day, it is vital that this sleep is of good quality. Unfortunately, the stresses and sensory overload endemic in modern life mean that sleeplessness is becoming an increasing problem. Added to this is the fact that we have, on average, an hour and a half less sleep per night than our predecessors a century ago. The result is an impairment of our mental faculties, our emotional balance, and our ability to fight disease.

Creating a comfortable sleeping environment is essential for achieving good-quality sleep. The bedroom should be the quietest room in the home—a protected space in which we can find stillness, soothed by gentle lighting and soft, luxurious furnishings. Pervading the room may be an air of romance, for it is here that we spend our most intimate moments.

Transform your bedroom into a retreat from the pressures of the modern world: introduce antique furnishings to reconnect with the past;

banish electrical items, such as televisions and computers, for these not only obstruct the drift to sleep by exciting the senses, but also generate electromagnetic fields that cause restlessness and disturbed sleep. If noise from neighbors or adjacent rooms is a problem, install some built-in cupboards along the adjoining wall to absorb the sound.

The bed is the focus of the bedroom and a crucial factor in determining the quality of our sleep. It should be proportionate in size to that of the room and able to accommodate its occupants with ease. A supportive mattress that molds to the contours of your body will promote restful sleep and guard against back problems. If possible, position the bed so that your head points south. According to Vedic tradition, the body, like the earth, has an electromagnetic field, with the head as the north pole. If you sleep with your head pointing north, the north pole of your head repels that of the earth, causing energy disturbances that disrupt sleeping patterns.

softness

"The softest thing
in the world can
ride roughshod
over the hardest
in the world."

Lao Zi

The bedroom provides a quiet haven for restful sleep and the design of the interior should reflect this function. Introduce soft, seductive shapes into your bedroom with draped throws and an abundance of cushions in cozy textures. The scattering of cushions in the bedrooms shown above creates a sense of warmth and luxury that encourages relaxation and surrender to sleep. To soften the lighting hang drapes or blinds at the windows, and install dimmable lights overhead and low-wattage lamps by the bedside. Candles and gossamer muslin drapes, such as those in the bedroom opposite, give the dreamlike effect of tranquil, muted light.

Invest in bedlinen made from soft, natural fibers, such as Egyptian cotton, silk, and fine linen, which will allow your skin to breathe during the night. Have some extra pillows and cushions for night-time reading, but sleep with just one firm pillow to support your neck.

Aromas are nature's aphrodisiacs. The essence of roses was used by the Romans to make love potions. To exalt the mind, perfume the room with fresh flowers or essential oils— the potent fragrance of hyacinths, the allure of ylang-ylang oil.

romance

Bedrooms provide the setting for some of our most intimate moments. Bringing an air of romance to the interior design of a bedroom can enhance these moments with a partner, nurturing passion and sensuality. A four-poster bed dressed with white, translucent drapes appeals to the romantic imagination with its overtones of fairytale princesses and castles in the clouds. If you lack space for a four-poster bed, suspend a muslin drape or mosquito net from the ceiling over your existing bed—the effect will be equally enchanting.

Whites, creams, dusky pinks, and lilacs have romantic affinities, forming an ideal color scheme for a bedroom. For fabrics choose muted patterns with soft edges that blur the distinction between fantasy and reality. Turn off overhead lights and rely instead on low-wattage and indirect lamps and uplighters. Warm-colored lampshades are particularly effective because they produce a flattering rosy glow. Aromas are natural aphrodisiacs, so perfume the room with scent-rich flowers, such as jasmine, or essential oils, such as rose and neroli. Alternatively, simply open up the windows, inviting cooling breezes to freshen your room.

"Do not seek to follow in the footsteps of the ancient ones; seek what they sought."

Basho

old and new

Juxtaposing the old and the new brings a home into the present moment, providing a link between the accumulated wisdom of the past and the innovation of today. It is the perfect marriage for the bedroom, for this is where memories of past and present are fused in the rich mosaic of dreams. Antique pieces painted in the neutral tones of modern minimalism (such as the wardrobe above) impart an element of history to an interior without excessive nostalgia for times past. Treating surfaces with distressed finishes can temper the newness of modern furniture: crackle glazes work well on painted wooden furniture; green and bronze finishes imitate verdigris on metal or ceramics. Setting an elaborate ornament typical of previous eras (such as the mantelpiece clock opposite) against the plainer interiors of today makes for a lively eclecticism, while introducing classic pieces into any room creates a look that is at once old and new. Handcrafted items possess this kind of timeless appeal, for they have an individuality that outlasts the fluctuating tides of fashion.

stillness

"Contemplate motion
in stillness and
stillness in motion,
both stillness and
movement disappear."

Sosan Zenji

Although many sleep experts advise that the bedroom should be reserved for sleeping and lovemaking, in busy family households your bedroom may offer your only chance of solitude and quiet rest or reflection. If this is the case, have something in your bedroom on which to sit or lie during periods of contemplation—perhaps a chair (above) or a hammock (opposite). Devote the bed to sleep and lovemaking alone.

During your period of reflection, there should be something inspiring on which to rest your gaze. If your bedroom overlooks a garden, face toward the window. Watch the fluttering of the leaves on the trees, treating them as a focus for meditation. Alternatively, create a focal point within the bedroom with a treasured painting or a sculpture. If you are reclining in a rocking chair or hammock, close your eyes and allow the gentle sway to lull your senses and still your thoughts.

proportion

Proportion means a perfect balance between space and form. Although important in every room of the home, a sense of proportion is particularly crucial in the master bedroom, where it helps to maintain the fine balance between intimacy and personal space.

Bedrooms that are small or have low or slanted ceilings can sometimes feel claustrophobic. To increase the sense of space in such rooms, minimize clutter and choose furniture that is correspondingly small or low in size, such as the bed and bedside tables in the bedroom above.

On the other hand, bedrooms that are extremely large can sometimes leave us feeling lost and isolated. To foster a cozier, more intimate atmosphere, divide up the room into smaller areas using paper or fabric screens, or a free-standing wall (opposite). Either opt for a high, large-framed bed, or elevate your existing bed on a platform to give it greater prominence in the room. Another strategy is to install built-in cupboards along one of the walls. This will make the room appear and feel smaller as well as providing additional storage space for clothes, shoes and accessories.

diffusion

In cities many of us live in a surreal landscape of perpetual light, our nights disturbed by the orange glow of streetlights filtering through bedroom drapes. Reinforcing the natural cycles of light and dark in our bedrooms can help to promote more restful sleep (our bodies regulate our sleeping patterns according to levels of light). Hang translucent fabrics or Venetian blinds (opposite) at the windows, or install sand-blasted glass windowpanes to diffuse evening light, creating a twilight that prepares the mind for sleep. Install lights with dimmer switches that you can turn up gradually in the morning—a gentle way to start the day. Be imaginative with your light fittings: light emanating from behind a headboard (above) mimics light as it streams over the horizon at sunrise.

"In the whole world there

is nothing softer

And weaker than water.

And yet nothing measures

up to it

In the way it works upon

that which is hard."

Lao Zi

BATHROOMS

cleansing spaces

The bathroom is a place for the cleansing and regeneration of body, mind, and spirit. It is home to our daily rituals of purification, of invigorating showers and relaxing baths. Central to the nature and function of the bathroom is water—an element traditionally deemed sacred for its unique powers to cleanse and heal, soothe and stimulate. A peaceful bathroom environment is one that supports and reflects the vital properties of water: it is a haven of purity, scrupulously clean and clutter-free, disturbed only by the melodic sounds of water as it gushes from the shower or the faucets.

Rooms with generous windows make ideal bathrooms because they have a lightness and airiness that is healing to the mind and emotions. Opening the windows of the bathroom also has a purifying effect, allowing the condensation that collects during bathing and showering to dissipate, thereby preventing the growth of mildew. An extractor fan will perform the same role and is essential in a bathroom without windows. Purify and freshen the air with the natural fragrances of essential oils (rather than synthetic air fresheners, which contain harmful chemicals). Try a stimulating scent, such as geranium, to rouse you in the morning, and a relaxing oil, such as lavender or jasmine, to promote unwinding at night.

Install a flexible lighting scheme that can promote both stimulation and relaxation. Fix a bright light over a mirror for shaving and applying cosmetics, with dimmable overhead spotlights on a separate circuit. This combination will enable you to adjust the brightness of the light according to your mood, task, and the time of day.

When we are in the bathroom we are generally barefoot, so it is important to pay careful consideration to the flooring. Smooth stone or marble flags are good—they are water-resistant and possess a roughness of texture that guards against slipping. If you prefer something warmer underfoot, opt for a natural, durable material, such as sisal or seagrass matting.

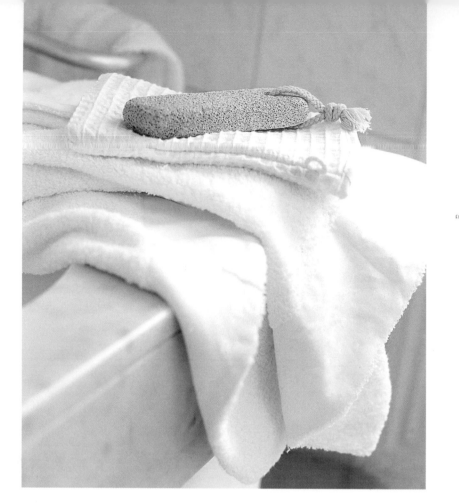

"The moment you have in your heart this extraordinary thing called 'pureness', you will discover that for you the world is transformed."

Krishnamurti

purity

Purity is the perfect theme for uniting the esthetics and design of the bathroom, extending the physical process of purification to encompass our mental, emotional, and spiritual levels, too. White is the color most often associated with purity. Used throughout the bathroom for walls, drapes or blinds, and bathroom units, white bestows a look of almost monastic ascetism that promotes mental clarity. However, an all-white bathroom can be overwhelming. To temper the starkness introduce neutral shades—perhaps a pale gray marble bathtub (above), untreated woodwork, or biscuit surfaces (opposite).

To enhance the visual purity and general cohesion of your bathroom interior, focus on a single shape and echo it in each of your units and their

fittings. In the bathroom shown opposite, the shape of the bathtub (straight with curved ends) is mirrored in the elegant forms of the metal faucets, the showerhead, and the shower rail above. Try to match the shapes of basins and mirrors, too. The symmetrical forms of geometric shapes, such as ovals, circles, rectangles, and squares, are most effective. To take the symmetry one step further, opt for a bathtub that has the faucets and the plugs located in the center (above).

Aim for a relatively spartan look throughout the bathroom interior to highlight the simplicity of the forms. Limit bathroom units to essential pieces and conceal bathroom clutter in low, discreet cupboards. The exceptions to this rule are fluffy, white towels, which you should display in an accessible place (above). Ideally these towels should be made from natural fibers, such as cotton or linen—highly absorbent, porous fabrics that dry the skin gently yet effectively.

simple storage

Our bathrooms are often small rooms in which we house a large amount of paraphernalia, ranging from bulky towels and bathrobes to soaps, sponges, and endless beauty products. One way to make the most of the space available is to transform simple storage solutions into artistic features. Rather than concealing towels in cupboards, you could display them on a ladder-style rack inclined against the wall or arrange them neatly on open shelves (right). For a more spontaneous effect, erect a Shaker-style pegrail along one wall, or place some extra hooks on the back of the door to provide hanging space for clothes, towels, and bathrobes. Hardware stores often sell stacks of rush or wicker baskets, which you can suspend on chains from the ceiling. If wall-space is limited, these provide useful homes for soaps, sponges, brushes, and loofahs.

However they are displayed, certain bathroom supplies, such as medicines, toilet rolls, and cleaning products, will never look attractive. Store these out of sight in elegant cabinets, or closed units that blend in with the rest of the interior. Cabinets with mirrored doors (above) can make good, space-providing alternatives to straightforward mirrors.

"The moon

abiding in the midst of

a tranquil mind;

clouds break

into light."

Dogen

tranquillity

A long soak in a warm bath is one of the best ways to relax at the end of a busy day, allowing the gentle caress of the water to soothe your body and calm your mind and emotions. To ensure that your bathing experience is always a comfortable one, install a large bath in which you can recline at full stretch. Locate the faucets in the center of the bath, rather than at one end, so that you do not have to stretch far to reach them. Baths that are either elevated or sunken, and accessed by a flight of steps (up or down), emphasize the sacred nature of bathing. Climbing up to the bath (opposite) is a symbol of spiritual ascent; the act of descending into water recalls bathing rituals in sacred Hindu rivers, such as the Ganges.

If possible locate your bathtub adjacent to a window if it has a calming view of nature. If your bathroom lacks such a view, incorporate natural elements in the bathroom, such as plants and stones, seashells, and natural sponges. To create a truly relaxing ambiance, light your bathroom with softly glowing wall-lamps or lit candles. These remind us of the moon, which, according to Hindu philosophy, influences the body at deep physical, mental, and emotional levels, helping us to bring relaxation to every aspect of our being.

fluidity

According to Chinese philosophy, moving water possesses an abundance of *chi* (vital energy)—a quality experienced first-hand when we take a revitalizing shower or run our hands under a faucet. With its sparkling appearance and tinkling sound, flowing water also energizes interiors and provides a particularly appropriate theme for the bathroom—a space of invigoration as well as relaxation. If you can do so, position your shower with a window as its backdrop, as shown opposite. The cascading water from your shower will send rainbows dancing around the bathroom, like ribbons of positive energy. Complement this effect with an abundance of reflective surfaces, such as glass, metal, glazed tiles, marble, and mirrors. Tile your bathroom in the fragmented patterns of blue mosaics (above right). Recreate the spectacular cascades of natural waterfalls with faucets (above left) that protrude horizontally from the wall over flat-bottomed sinks.

"Map difficult

through easy.

Broach great

through narrow."

Lao Zi

HALLWAYS, LANDINGS, AND STAIRCASES

linking spaces

Hallways, landings, and staircases constitute the transitional zones of the home. They connect the different areas together, mediating our movement between inside and outside, one room and another, upstairs and downstairs. Although these areas are often marginalized in terms of design, our experiences when passing through them are extremely important because they color our impressions of the home as a whole. Ensuring that hallways, landings, and staircases are attractive, welcoming, and conducive to free movement is therefore essential for establishing a general sense of peacefulness within the home.

Before passing into the hallway, visitors to the home must cross the threshold of the front door. In Vedic tradition the front door is understood in terms of its dual role of welcoming positive energies into the home and providing protection from negative outside influences. Accordingly, a talisman is positioned over the front door to ward off evil spirits, and a Toran—

an embroidered, mirrorwork fabric—is hung around the door frame to shower good luck and blessings on all those who enter the home. Think of your front door in a similar way: ensure that it is solid and firm, with effective locks to protect you from burglary; and paint it in a bright, attractive color to welcome guests into your home.

As your guests pass through the front door, greet them with a light, welcoming, and well-organized hallway that ushers them into the home. Assign space in which to remove and store outdoor shoes so that dirt from outside does not pollute the interior. Erect a pegrail for hanging coats and bags to avoid cluttering up the floor of the hallway.

Landings and staircases should also be kept clear of obstructions to facilitate movement between different rooms and floors. Often regarded as dead spaces, these areas are in fact ideal settings for displaying paintings, sculptures, and collections of books.

openness

The hallway gives visitors their first impressions of your home, so it is important to conjure an atmosphere of warmth and welcome that embraces them into your personal space. To create this sense of openness, ensure that your hallway is light, bright, and clear. Hallways with high ceilings and large windows or skylights are ideal because they are blessed with an abundance of natural light and possess a natural sense of expansion (above right). In hallways that are dark and narrow, you can contrive the effect of openness by painting the walls in light, refreshing colors, such as whites, creams, pale blues, greens, and yellows, and illuminating the space with bright full-spectrum lighting.

Wooden (above left) or sandstone (opposite) floors imbue hallways with a welcoming warmth, while a narrow rug or painted strip running the length of the hallway (above right) draws visitors into the home. An arrangement of flowers or potted plants placed near the door issues a cheerful greeting and softens the transition between outdoors and indoors.

transition

Hallways, landings, and stairways are transitory spaces, for they are the circulation routes that connect one area of the home to another. We can compare them to the meridians (energy channels that, according to traditional Chinese medicine, link the different parts of the body)—both must be kept clear of blockages to permit energy to flow freely. For this reason it is important to keep oversized furniture or unnecessary junk to a minimum, particularly in modest homes that have narrow corridors and low ceilings. One option is to install discreet cupboards for the storage of items, such as shoes, hats, and coats.

The extended wall-spaces of hallways, landings, and stairways are also ideal locations for the display of artworks or collections of books. When arranging these items group them according to visual themes, such as color or style. In the landing shown opposite, black-and-white photographs provide a thematic thread linking one space to another in a dynamic visual rhythm.

level crossings

Staircases provide us with a means to traverse the different levels of the home, but unlike elevators (which can seem claustrophobic) they give us a stronger sensation of traveling through space. To render this experience a smooth and enjoyable one, ensure that your staircases have wide treads and supporting banisters. Wooden treads (below left) are grounding and give a sense of security; those constructed from glass (below right) and stainless steel (opposite) are ideal if your priority is to maximize the flow of light. Your staircase should enhance rather than dominate your interior: in small areas elegant spiral staircases, or staircases without visible supports, create a sense of expansion and movement but occupy minimal space; in larger interiors wide, sweeping staircases chime with the more imposing nature of the space.

"The Great Path has no gate,

thousands of roads enter it.

When one passes through

this gateless gate,

One walks freely between

heaven and earth."

Mumon

ONE-ROOM LIVING: LOFTS AND STUDIOS

open spaces

With the rise of modern technology—the advent of the computer and the mobile telephone—the boundaries between our public and private lives are becoming increasingly blurred. This shift is reflected in the modern trend for living in one-room homes, such as lofts and studios, in which the different areas of the home are elements of a single open space.

One-room living is largely an urban phenomenon—a response to the increasing cost of living space in overcrowded cities. Converted from disused factories and warehouses, lofts are generally located on urban fringes or along urban waterways. Large spaces, with expansive windows and high ceilings, lofts were originally the preserve of artists, who found them apt settings for both living and working. As increasing numbers gravitated toward long-derelict industrial zones, these areas were transformed into lively communities, with the result that loft-living has become an ever-more stylish and popular option for young city dwellers. By contrast, studios are usually created by splitting old houses into flats. They are therefore smaller and more compact than lofts, and tend to be located in city centers.

The lack of dividing walls in one-room homes means that, regardless of size, they are generally light and airy. Understood in terms of Eastern traditions, their openness allows energy to flow freely through them, making them particularly vibrant places in which to live. Design schemes for a one-room living space should seek to preserve this feature by emphasizing the sense of space and the structure that contains it.

Any approach to the interior design of a loft or studio also needs to take into account the singularity of the space, as well as its diverse nature: on one hand, the principle of unity should be applied to the home as a whole to infuse an overall sense of cohesion throughout the space; on the other hand, the design scheme should be sufficiently flexible to accommodate and distinguish between the areas dedicated to particular activities.

"To see oneness
in all beings
And undivided
wholeness in
all manifold
shapes:
Know that to be
the true light."

Bhagavad Gita

expansion

The openness of lofts and studios gives them an innate sense of expansion. This has a liberating effect on the occupants, fostering joyfulness and self-expression. We can cultivate expansion in a number of different ways. Emphasize space over form by storing clutter in discreet cupboards and avoiding heavy or bulky furniture. Opt for a limited number of delicate pieces of furniture: perhaps a modern glass table and streamlined metal chairs (above); or, for a period look, the simple elegance of antique furniture (opposite).

Large windows or skylights increase the sense of openness by letting light flood into the room. To maximize the flow of light, paint walls, ceilings, and floors in pale, muted colors, and install large mirrors to bounce the light around the room and create the illusion of extended space.

structure

In many cases the unique character of a loft or studio derives from the raw-edged solidity of exposed structural features, such as open ceilings, beams, and pillars—the legacy of an industrial past. Highlighting these features through design helps us to appreciate the essential nature of the home.

In the loft shown opposite, the spotlights are angled upward to emphasize the striking octagonal structure and geometric beamwork of the ceiling. In the loft shown above, it is the fabric of the walls that forms the main point of focus, in a strong textural interplay between the roughness of the exposed brickwork (the window alcoves) and the smooth, civilized surfaces of plaster walls.

To balance their stress on the solidity and structure of ceilings and walls, both interiors boast floors colored in expansive shades of blue. The result is an exhilarating inversion of the world as we know it, with the earth above and the heavens below. It is a defamiliarization that awakens our perception, teaching us to look at our surroundings afresh.

dividing lines

The challenge of living in a single space is finding ways to demarcate the different areas designated for cooking, eating, bathing, and sleeping, without compromising openness. Movable folding screens, made from fabric, paper, or wood, offer the greatest flexibility. Rattan or translucent shades, or drapes, hanging on rails from the ceiling (below), provide an alternative. Paper shades or thin, pale drapes allow light to filter through into the rest of the room.

If your living space has high ceilings, you may be able to add a mezzanine, giving additional floor space and a private area for sleeping or working (opposite). If this is impossible,

try elevating or lowering the floor in certain areas—creating perhaps a raised bed or a sunken bath to add variety and make subtle divisions within the space.

Less radical options include the use of different types of flooring to distinguish between particular areas. For example, you could lay tiles in the kitchen area and sisal in the bedroom area, establishing a division between the two based on textural opposites. Placing different rugs in individual areas has a similar effect.

The positioning of furniture is perhaps the easiest way to define individual areas. Install free-standing shelving units to mark obvious distinctions between different parts of the home. To create a cozy seating area, set sofas and chairs in an L or U shaped formation, and use lamps cited strategically to highlight the area (right).

"When I step out, the world

assembles itself around me

Like my awareness of being

who I am."

Anonymous

ordering chaos

In a one-room living space, every area of your life is on view, so it is important to find interesting and attractive ways in which to display your possessions. This is particularly the case with miscellaneous objects—items without an obvious place within the home, whose presence can be a physical obstruction as well as mental distraction if they are not stored according to principles of order.

The shelves shown opposite and cubbyholes shown left are set into the walls, ensuring that objects do not intrude upon the rooms. The clean geometry of their gridlike forms is visually arresting and provides a framework within which the objects can be organized into groups, according to esthetic principles, such as type, size, shape, or color. The objects set against the stark whiteness of the cubbyholes project forward into view; those arranged on the dark brown shelves emerge only partially from the gloom—a seemingly organic part of the unit.

cohesion

When all the different aspects of the home are contained within a single room it is best to develop a design scheme that unifies the disparate areas of the home into a single cohesive unit. As we have seen previously (see pages 34–5), unity is established through the dynamic interplay of opposites: in the picture shown right, bands of light alternate with shade; in the picture shown left, black interacts with white; soft, woollen bedcovers are offset by the hard, shiny floor; and a square fireplace and linear chairs contrast with the circular shape of the table and the rounded form of the egg.

This interplay of difference not only banishes monotony, but also allows for the expression of the unique qualities of specific areas within the overriding unity of the room. For example, in the sleeping area the stark black and white of the color scheme transmute into shades of brown and cream to convey the softness characteristic of a bedroom; in the eating area the whiteness of the interior provides a dazzling backdrop for a vase of red flowers, whose flash of vibrant color evokes the convivial atmosphere of a dining room.

"The natural world is
subject as well as
object. The natural
world is the maternal
source of our being."

Thomas Berry

GARDENS,
BALCONIES,
AND DECKS

outdoor spaces

Spending time exposed to the gentle, harmonizing influences of nature is one of the simplest ways to regain a sense of peace. Yet for many of us, who live amid the concrete and asphalt of urban landscapes, the natural world is all too often a distant dream. Cut off from nature in this way, we develop a sense of rootlessness and isolation, an unsettling feeling of complete separation from the world around us.

Cultivating a garden can help to heal this fractured sense of self by bringing us into direct contact with the five basic elements essential to life— earth, air, water, sunlight, and space. This experience reminds us of our fundamental connection to all other life forms, of our place as integral parts in an interdependent web of relations. It is a revelation that brings a sense of wholeness and belonging, a discovery of home.

We tend to think of gardens exclusively in terms of large outdoor spaces that have been beautifully landscaped, with extensive lawns, trees, and flowerbeds. In fact, a garden can be created in almost any outdoor space —on a rooftop or balcony, and even in a windowbox. All that is needed is fertile soil, access to sunlight and water, and sufficient space in which to grow. Before planting assess the balance of elements in your garden and choose varieties of plants that will flourish in the conditions present. For example, for a windowbox located on a shaded side of the house, select small plants that prefer shade to direct sunshine.

The design principles that form the basis of harmonious interiors can also be applied to the garden. The key in both cases is to devise a simple, unified design scheme, founded on a balance between space and form, light and dark, complemented by a range of different textures and a harmonious color scheme. When this is achieved we create a garden that appeals to all the senses, gently opening our awareness to the soothing and vital presence that pervades all living things.

mystery

The garden is a place for exploration and discovery—a part of the home where we can engage with and feel part of the natural world where we belong. Gardens that possess an air of mystery draw us in with promises of revelation and surprise, encouraging us to regain our receptivity to the wisdom of nature.

In the garden shown left, the intriguing curves of a flight of steps capture the imagination, drawing us into the garden. Red and purple flowers here and there punctuate the green with shots of surprising intensity; beyond the arbor tantalizing glimpses of an open space beckon us to explore. Hazy sunshine filters through the shrubbery, infusing the scene with a mysterious, almost magical quality.

If you prefer clean geometric shapes to organic curves, use the irregularity of asymmetry to create a balance that is both dynamic and surprising. For example, in the garden shown opposite, the structured look of box hedging and topiary is given a surprising twist when juxtaposed with a pathway, whose eccentric meanderings entice the eye toward the mysterious darkness at the end of the garden.

juxtaposition

The careful juxtaposition of contrasting textures, shapes, and colors is as important in the garden as it is in the home. Such juxtapositions not only appeal to our senses, they also draw our attention to the uniqueness of individual forms as well as to the relativity of this uniqueness, which is entirely dependent upon the relationships between one form and another.

There are many different ways to achieve contrasts. Smooth, green foliage set against the warmth and roughness of red terracotta pots and the cool, bluish-gray mesh of a perforated fence (opposite) creates a lively interplay of color and texture. Twisted green shoots winding around a lattice fence (above right) suggest a balance between the seeming chaos of nature and the ordering impulse of humankind. Old metal watering cans (above left) contrast with the canopy of fresh new growth, reminding us of the processes of change that affect all things, whether natural or manmade.

calming water

An abundance of water is essential to a vital, energized garden: it purifies and ionizes the air, enables plants to absorb and utilize nutrients from the soil, and attracts a welcome variety of wildlife. Strengthen the presence of this element within your garden by installing a stylish water feature, such as a fountain or a pond. Locate it in a prominent position, visible from your windows, to act as an important focal point for the garden (below).

Stepping stones or wooden decking laid across a pond help us to interact more directly with the water element. For example, in the garden shown opposite, a large pond is spanned by a curved walkway. This allows us to appreciate the water feature from a variety of different perspectives and permits us close proximity with both the calming stillness of the pond and the energizing flow of the fountain. The curve of the walkway is mirrored in the

"Follow the stream,
have faith in its
course. The water will
go on its own way,
meandering here and
there. It will find the
grooves, cracks and
crevices. Just follow
the stream. Never let
it out of your sight."

Sheng Yen

interconnecting swathes of underwater stone and the floating algae that pattern the surface of the pond in a way that is strikingly reminiscent of the circular ripples of water.

The image of the fountain and the pond provides a metaphor for life: the ceaselessly flowing water suggesting action, the quiet stillness of the pond evoking contemplation. According to ancient Chinese philosophy, action and contemplation are the attributes of the King and the Sage, and represent the two key aspects of a balanced life. In the West emphasis is placed on action at the expense of contemplation. To restore the balance in your own life, it can help to spend some time sitting quietly in contemplation on a bench or chair adjacent to a pond. To create a focal point for your meditation, try gazing at your reflection in the water, seeing yourself made whole in another dimension, a separate being, yet inextricably linked to your surroundings. Alternatively, grow some exquisite pink and white waterlilies, such as those shown above, on the surface of the pond. As you focus on their delicate forms, take a moment to appreciate their existence as a manifestation of the abundance and beauty of the natural world—a world of which each one of us is an integral part.

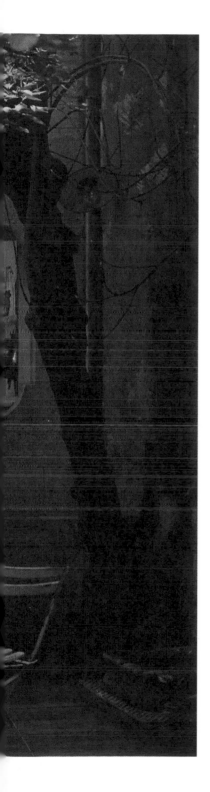

inside outside

Courtyards, conservatories, and walled gardens combine the privacy and seclusion of interiors with the openness of the outdoors, bridging the divide between inside and outside. Essentially they are outdoor rooms, enclosed spaces in which we can enjoy the benefits of nature—warm sunshine, an abundance of plantlife—undisturbed by the vagaries of the weather, the prying eyes of neighbors, the noise and bustle of the outside world. The outdoor room shown above has been created by sectioning off the area around an outside door. Wicker screens enclose the space, applying the artifice of interiors to the fabric and textures of nature.

An outdoor room is an extension of the home. In the courtyard shown opposite, the interior of the home is clearly visible through the large French windows, blurring the boundary between inside and out. The courtyard itself is comfortable and roomlike, the roughness of the ground concealed beneath smooth wooden floorboards, the table and chairs providing a quiet place to rest in the warmth of the sunshine, beneath the shade of a tree.

outside dining

The garden offers the perfect setting for dining, morning, noon, and night. Outdoors, away from the distractions of the telephone and the television, you can eat at leisure, able to appreciate not only the flavors of your meal, but also the fundamental connection between what you are eating and its source in the natural world.

Patios, balconies, and verandas are the most obvious locations for outside dining, as these supply a firm, stable surface on which to set a table and chairs. For outdoor breakfasts and lunches it is important to provide some shade above the dining table. In the patio shown opposite, white canvas sheets strung up above the table make a

"How long the stars

Have been fading,

The lamplight dimming:

There's neither coming,

Nor going."

Nansen

stunning open canopy. Billowing casually, the sheets echo the exuberant informality of the table arrangement, which comprises white, frothy daisies growing in earthy terracotta pots. In contrast, Thai-style bamboo screens (page 162) create a more exotic effect that evokes the tropical climes of Asia. Shielding diners from the glare of the sun, the bamboo screens fence off a secluded, intimate dining area that is refreshed by gentle breezes filtering through the slats.

An outdoor evening soirée can be a magical occasion. To evoke an air of mystery, dispense with artificial lighting and instead use myriad candles to illuminate the dining area—their gentle flickering glow echoes the luminescence of the moon, bestowing a diffused effect that is more in keeping with the natural surroundings. To avoid candles being extinguished by breezes and to prevent any accidents, place tealights or floating candles in bowls or glasses filled with water. If you are feeling more extravagant, you could invest in some pretty lanterns: either arrange one or two in the center of the table, or hang a series of smaller lanterns from nearby trees, or the eaves of the balcony or veranda; as they sway in the breeze they will cast flickering shadows, which will bring a sense of dynamic movement to the occasion.

"Nothing can bring you lasting peace;
you have it already if you just stop
disturbing it."

Swami Satchidananda

seclusion

The perfect place in which to reconnect with your inner
peacefulness is a tranquil, secluded part of your garden.
Sitting here you can truly begin to relax, opening your
senses to the caress of fresh air, the melodious sounds of
chirruping birds and leaves rustling in the breeze, and the
fragrant scents and vibrant blooms of flowers. Soothed by
nature in this way, we can let go of habitual worries and
begin to feel more grounded and calm.

Look for a quiet, shady spot from which you can view
your garden. The dappled shade offered by trees (opposite)
is ideal, as this allows some light to filter through, ensuring

that the shade does not seem oppressive. The arbor shown below is covered with a dense canopy of creepers and plants. Resting here, surrounded by plantlife on all sides, we become absorbed in the garden. A quiet spot on a balcony or veranda (opposite) can be very conducive to moments of contemplation because its elevated position will often furnish an overview of the surrounding area, giving you a valuable sense of perspective.

In your chosen outdoor location, position a bench or chair, and possibly a small table. Furniture of wood or stone will be in keeping with the natural setting, ageing in tandem with the ebb and flow of the seasons. Stone is particularly hardwearing, with a solidity and weight that enhances the stillness of the space. Wood is lighter and therefore gives you the freedom to alter the position of your bench or chair as you please.

"There is something
infinitely healing in
the repeated refrains
of nature – the
assurance that dawn
comes after the night
and spring after
the winter."

Rachel Carson

index

acknowledgments

Picture credits

The publishers would like to thank the following people and photographic libraries for permission to reproduce their material. Every care has been taken to trace copyright holders. However, if we have omitted anyone we apologize for this and will, if informed, make corrections in any future edition.

1 Red Cover/Winfried Heinze/architects Studio Azzurro; 5 Vega MG/Gianni Basso/architect Jim Gillam/interior designer Jane Laidley; 10-11 The Interior Archive/Eduardo Munoz/designer Kelly Hoppen; 15 The Interior Archive/Eduardo Munoz/designer Kelly Hoppen; 16 Guy Obijn/architect Piet Boon; 17 Guy Obijn/architect Carlo Seminck; 19 Sanoma Syndication/Otto Polman; 23 Red Cover/Graham Atkins-Hughes; 24 Ray Main/Mainstream; 25 Camera Press/Sarie Vaisi; 26 Vega MG/Eugeni Pons/architect Anne Bugnani; 30 Red Cover/Reto Guntli/designer Lilia Konrad; 31 Deco Idées/Laurent Brandajs; 33 Red Cover/Chris Evans; 35 The Interior Archive/Fritz von der Schulenburg/designer Mimmi O'Connell; 36-37 Paul Ryan/International Interiors/designer Jacqueline Morabito; 40 left Sanoma Syndication/Hotze Eisma; 40 right Verne Photography/design Obumex; 41 Narratives/Jan Baldwin/architect Jonathan Clark; 42 IPC Syndication/© Homes & Gardens/Pia Tryde; 43 Red Cover/© Maisons Coté Sud/Bernard Touillon; 44-45 Vega MG/Giorgio Possenti/architect Vincent van Duysen; 46 Ray Main/Mainstream; 47 Vega MG/Giulio Oriani/architect Clara Bona; 48 Vega MG/Giulio Oriani/architect Andrew Meriring; 49 Vega MG/Giulio Oriani/architect Clara Bona/Studio 98; 50-51 Vega MG/Giulio Oriani/architect Arthur Quinton; 52-53 Ray Main/Mainstream; 54 Narratives/Jan Baldwin; 55 Christian Sarramon; 56 left The Interior Archive/Ed Reeve; 56 right Ray Main/Mainstream; 57 Red Cover/Ken Hayden; 58 above Red Cover/Graham Atkins-Hughes/architect Sally Vogel; 58 below Undine Pröhl/architect Rob Quigley; 59 Paul Ryan/International Interiors/designer Jacqueline Morabito; 60-61 The Interior Archive/Eduardo Munoz/designer Kelly Hoppen; 64 Red Cover/© Maison Coté Sud/Erick Saillet; 65 IPC Syndication/© Living Etc./Paul Massey; 66 left View/Peter Cook/Tugman Architects; 66 right Ray Main/Mainstream; 67 Verne Photography; 68 Vega MG/Giorgio Possenti/architect Hilde Cornelissen; 69 Lars Hallén/Design Press; 70-71 Jan Verlinde/architect Vincent van Duysen; 72 Red Cover/Jake Fitzjones/Fulham Kitchens; 73 Ray Main/Mainstream; 74 The Interior Archive/Edina van der Wyck; 75 Red Cover/© Maison Coté Sud/Erick Saillet; 76 Sanoma Syndication/Paul Grootes; 77 Vega MG/Giorgio Possenti; 78-79 Red Cover/Ken Hayden; 82 left Red Cover/Jake Fitzjones; 82 right Narratives/Jan Baldwin/house owned by the designers of Storm Watches; 83 Guy Obijn/architect Christel Peeters; 84 Sanoma Syndication/Bonita Postma; 85 Vega MG/Gianni Basso; 86-87 IPC Syndication/© Homes & Gardens/Russell Sadur; 88-89 The Interior Archive/Tim Beddow; 90 The Interior Archive/Andrew Wood; 91 Vega MG/Giorgio Possenti/architects Andrew Stanic & Andy Harding; 92 Deco Idées/Frédéric Raevens; 93 The Interior Archive/Fritz von der Schulenburg/architect Nico Rensch; 94-95 Vega MG/Guilio Oriani/architects Stefan Antoni & Mark Reilly; 96 Bruno Helbling/Karin Kern/Interior design Marco Carenini, Redbox; 97 Red Cover/Ken Hayden/architect John Pawson; 98-99 The Interior Archive/Luke White; 102 Ray Main/Mainstream; 103 The Interior Archive/Tim Clinch; 104 Red Cover/Winfried Heinze/designer Emily Todhunter; 105 Ray Main/Mainstream; 106 left Red Cover/Graham Atkins-Hughes; 106 right The Interior Archive/Andrew Wood; 107 Vega MG/Giorgio Possenti; 108 The Condé Nast Publications/Mikkel Vang, Courtesy Vogue Living, Australia; 109 The Condé Nast Publications/Geoff Lung, Courtesy Vogue Living, Australia; 110 Guy Obijn/architect André Martens; 111 The Interior Archive/Fritz von der Schulenburg/designer Mimmi O'Connell; 112-113 Red Cover/Ken Hayden/architect John Pawson; 114 left Camera Press/Sarie Visi; 114 right Red Cover/James Mitchell; 115 Red Cover/© Maisons Coté Sud/Erick Saillet; 116-117 Red Cover/Winfried Heinze; 120 Red Cover/© Maisons Coté Sud/Erick Saillet; 121 left Red Cover/Ken Hayden; 121 right Red Cover/Verity Welstead; 122 Red Cover/Ken Hayden/architect Collett Zarzycki; 123 Red Cover/Brian Harrison; 124-125 Vega MG/Giulio Oriani/architects Stefan Antoni & Greg Wright; 126 Bruno Helbling/Mirko Beetschen/architect Frei Architekten; 127 left View/Chris Gascoigne/Cogswell Horne Architects; 127 right Vega MG/Giulio Oriani/architects Stefan Antoni & Greg Wright; 128-129 Red Cover/© Maisons Coté Sud/Pere Planells; 132 Red Cover/Graham Atkins-Hughes/architect Nik Randall; 133 Red Cover/Andreas von Einsiedel/designer Jorn Langberg; 134 Paul Ryan/International Interiors/designer Scott Bromley; 135 The Interior Archive/Fritz von der Schulenburg/architect Nico Rensch; 136 Narratives/Jan Baldwin/designed by the owner, food writer and creative director, Alastair Hendy; 137 Marie Claire Maison/Vincent Leroux/Jean Oddes/José Postic; 138 Didier Delmas/designer Frédéric Méchiche; 139 Red Cover/Ken Hayden/designer Jonathan Reed; 140-141 Scott Frances/designer Stephen Roberts/lighting designer Cooley Monato Studios/construction Dutchman Contracting Inc.; 142 Abode Interiors Picture Library/Trevor Richards/architect Ed Seymour; 143 Scott Frances/designer Stephen Roberts/lighting designer Cooley Monato Studios/construction Dutchman Contracting Inc.; 144-145 David Matheson/interior designer Nic Graham; 145 The Interior Archive/Andrew Wood; 146-147 Red Cover/Polly Farquharson/designer Ruth Aram; 150 Red Cover/Hugh Palmer; 151 Red Cover/Hugh Palmer; 152 Clive Nichols/Lisette Pleasance; 153 left Marcus Harpur/Glemham House, Suffolk; 153 right Nicola Browne/design David & Judy Drew; 154 Nicola Browne/designer Ron Lutsko, California; 155 Résidences Décoration/Alain Sauvan/garden designer Jean-Louis Cura/architect Marc Félix/artist Michele Schneider; 156 Christian Sarramon; 157 Nicola Browne; 158-159 Nicola Browne/Catherine Heatherington, London; 160-161 Maison Madame Figaro/Vincent Thibert; 161 Nicola Browne/designer Philippe Niez; 162 IPC Syndication/© Living Etc./Simon Whitmore; 163 The Interior Archive/Fritz von der Schulenburg/architect Nico Rensch; 164-165 Jerry Harpur/RHS Hampton Court Palace Flower Show; 166-167 Deco Idées/Serge Anton; 168 The Interior Archive/Andrew Wood; 169 IPC Syndication/© Homes & Gardens/Tom Leighton; 170 Jerry Harpur/design Keith Corlett, NYC; 171 Narratives/Tamsyn Hill.

Author's acknowledgments

I would like to thank Tim, for his love and support while writing this book, and for all the funny moments. I am forever grateful to my mother, Brenda, for reading through the text, and to my sister, Mandy, for her computer skills. I would especially like to thank Lucy Latchmore for editing and shaping the text into an inspiring book, and the rest of the team at DBP, particularly the Art Department, for the evocative images and beautiful design.